THE LOVE
that comes
FROM GOD

THE LOVE

that comes

FROM GOD

Reflections on the Family

Chiara Lubich

New City Press

New York   London   Manila

Published in the United States, Great Britain, and the Philippines by
New City Press, 202 Cardinal Rd., Hyde Park, NY 12538, U.S.A.
New City, 57 Twyford Ave., London W3 9PZ, England
New City Publications, 4800 Valenzuela St., Sta Mesa, 1016 Manila,
    Philippines

Translated from the original Italian edition
Una famiglia per rinnovare la società
©1993 Città Nuova Editrice

Cover design: Ave Center, Loppiano, Italy

Library of Congress Cataloging-in-Publication Data:

Lubich, Chiara, 1920-
    [Famiglia per rinnovare la società.   English.]
    The love that comes from God : reflections on the family / Chiara
    Lubich.

    ISBN 1-56548-030-9 (paper)
    1. Family—Religious life.   2. Catholic Church—Doctrines.
    I. Title.
    BX2351.L8313   1995
    248.4'82—dc20   95-20521

Printed in the United States of America

Contents

Introduction

In this remarkable book, the family is described as a treasure chest of love. I find this an evocative image. In my mind I see an old pirate's chest: not a cartoon picture of shimmering gold coins and sparkling jewels, but rather a battered old chest, misshapen and desperately in need of repair. When the lid is prised open, it is bursting at the seams with valuable odds and ends of so many different shapes and sizes. Perhaps the occasional diamond catches and refracts the light, but most of it is dusty and aged and in need of a vigorous scrub and polish.

This image is so apt for the family today. The family is, as ever, a priceless treasure, but in need of a good clean if it is to captivate and dazzle us in today's society. Not that all the changes in the world are bad, but the family in particular seems to be bearing the brunt of many of the new social and economic patterns. The strain leads to well-documented problems, such as the huge increase in divorces in this century, as well as the growing isolation experienced by many within their families, as nuclear families live apart from grandparents and each family member seems to become more and more caught up in the imperious demands of his or her own world.

If this is the case, then what is the polish, the secret ingredient needed to bring the family closer to its real glory? In order to begin to answer this question, we need to look at the context of the six talks contained within this book.

The book is made up of a series of talks which were given over a period of twelve years by Chiara Lubich, the founder and president of the Focolare Movement. Focolare began in 1943 in wartime Trent, Italy, when Chiara and her first companions began to understand that God, who is Love, was calling them to dedicate their lives in a particular way, to the fulfilment of Jesus' prayer: "Father, may they all be one" (John 17:21). Gathering many times a day in the uncertain safety of the air raid shelters, and face to face with death or injury, they became enchanted by the simplicity and radical nature of the Gospel message. Jesus' words leapt from each page as if they they had never been heard before. Phrases like: "Love one another as I have loved you"; "Love your enemies"; "Whatever you do to the least, you do to me" were taken to heart and immediately put into practice by these young girls. Unknown to this small group, something new was being born, a new light, a new way of life, a new gift of the Spirit, a charism, within the Church which can be summed up in one word: unity.

Unity, through the mutual love of this embryonic community, spread like a fire from Trent to the whole of Italy, and from Italy to all five continents. This fire could not be contained only within the Roman Catholic Church in which it was born, but eventually spread into other Christian denominations and has subsequently received the blessings of the leaders of the other major Churches. In fact, the fire has been so unquenchable that it has now even gone beyond the confines of the Churches, to believers of other faiths and to people with no specific religious commitment. It is in the discovery of what the fire of unity means that we begin to see possible answers for the needs of the family today.

Indeed there is a natural and deep connection between the Focolare and the family. Focolare means "the hearth," the traditional focal point of the family. In many ways Focolare is synonymous for family and therefore it is not surprising that Chiara Lubich speaks with such ardour. The first stirrings of unity within Trent saw people from all walks of life attracted to this first group of girls. There were lay and ordained, religious and married people, young and old from all social classes. All were linked by the desire to go to God not so much as isolated individuals but together, as a community.

These talks, then, are the fruit of a living experience and reflect a specific gift of the Spirit within the Church which is based on a collective rather than an individualistic spirituality. These words are addressed to people who want to live for God in unity, as one body. The family is made for such a spirituality: families, right from the first community in Trent, wanted to bring unity to the family, to ensure that all relationships are permeated with not just the natural love between members of a family, but also possess a supernatural dimension. In 1967, Chiara, seeing the tremendous wealth of experiences of the married members of the Focolare, launched the New Families Movement, with the specific aim of working toward the fulfilment of Jesus' prayer "That all may be one" through the work and witness of the family itself. Most of these talks were given at various congresses organized by the New Families on a variety of topics such as: education, prayer, society and the family.

I am conscious, as an Anglican, that Chiara Lubich is a Roman Catholic speaking to a mainly Roman Catholic audience. Not surprisingly, this colours what she says and how she says it. But it does not detract from the importance of her message. I hope, therefore, that this book will be read and treasured by all people interested in the world of the family. Even if occasionally someone from a different religious tradition might wish to phrase certain things differently, there really is something here for everybody. I was privileged to be present at four of these six talks, and was deeply impressed each time. They are rich in wisdom and are expressions of an authentic life which values all people, whatever their status or creed. They are, however, highly concentrated talks and will demand several readings, deep meditation and then of course they need to be lived. This is the challenge.

Paul Gateshill

The Treasure Chest of Love

It is quite useful to read this talk before the other five within this book. It sets the scene, because it deals with the underlying concern of everything that is said, that is, how the family can be built up and brought to its fulfilment by love.

The talk was given in 1981 at a weekend event, held in the vast Olympic Sports Stadium in Rome, the Palaeur. The event was called Familyfest and was a celebration of family life. Twenty thousand people, representing forty-nine nationalities, filled the stadium. The talk itself was the keynote speech to launch the whole weekend which was dedicated to the theme of "The Family and Love." This was followed by experiences of family life shared by people from all over the world.

In the afternoon of the same day, Pope John Paul II came to watch as the event unfolded with dance, music and more personal testimonies. He spoke, movingly for many of those present, including those who were not members of the Roman Catholic Church. He made a significant reference to the family as "the domestic Church," a comment in which he reminded everyone that when Jesus sent out his disciples, he sent them out two by two.

In her talk, however, Chiara speaks about the reality

of the family today in stark terms. But she does not stop there. Chiara goes on to invite the audience to consider God's view of the family as a treasure chest of love: containing all the different types of love which make up the many varied relationships within the family, maternal, paternal, filial and so on. Love then is at the heart of the family: "If the family has failed in the world, it is because love has diminished. When love dies out, the family disintegrates."

She illustrates how the family can be revitalized through a reinjection of love: not just an emotional love, but the love which Jesus is talking about when he commands his disciples to "love one another as I have loved you" (John 13:34 and 15:12).

The word "as" here is significant. Jesus loved to the point of giving his life on the cross. This is love at its peak, the climax of its self-giving. The family, with its natural, beautiful human love, a love which is mutual, is an obvious setting for the kind of love which Jesus demands. But it needs to become divinized, to be lived "as" Jesus has loved us. In this way it can reach its true fulfilment and perfection.

Love is thus the key to making the family what God intends it to be, a mirror of his own life. It is love which will renew relationships within the heart of each family. It is love too, which will open up each individual family to the needs of society around it, because as God is not closed in on himself, so the love of the family must spill outside of its own circle to embrace the needs of all around it.

The Family and Love

My dear friends, sisters and brothers, gathered here today from all over the world in the name of Jesus. May your hearts be overflowing with joy because of his presence.

Today we will be dealing with one of the most controversial topics we face at this moment in history, one of the most vital, disquieting topics of our times: the family.

What is the family?

But, what is the family? Sociologists, moralists, educators, politicians and psychologists could give a wide variety of definitions. I am convinced, however, that all of you are interested, above all, in one idea regarding the family: God's idea.

What is the family for God?

Today, during this gathering, we shall attempt to give an answer to this question. For the moment though, let us limit ourselves to making a simple observation.

In the act of creation, God formed a family. In becoming a man, God became part of a family. When Jesus began his mission, and manifested his glory, he was celebrating the formation of a new family. This alone should suffice to make us understand what the family is for God.

Today's family

But what is the family like today?

We all know the answer. The influence of harmful theories, the decline of traditional moral values, theoretical and concrete materialism, and the hedonistic mentality brought on by our consumer society have led, and continue to lead, a head-on attack against the family.

Above all, the libertarian and individualistic society has rendered the very idea of the indissolubility of marriage meaningless, and marriage is reduced to a mere "private act" free of all responsibility and commitment toward society.

We know how certain alarmist propaganda concerning over-population has led to a selfish and materialistic interpretation of the problem of "responsible parenthood" (which is, in itself, an important and serious matter). As a result, affluent societies, at this point, are tending toward a zero growth rate or even to a *decrease* in births as compared to deaths. And to have more than one child, or two at the most, is becoming out of the ordinary.

Weakening the family

We also know how the legislation of many nations tends to foster this decadent tendency, with laws that contribute toward weakening the stability of the family. Thus, we have divorce easily obtained, widespread abortion on demand, euthanasia, artificial contraception, male and female sterilization, inadequate economic aid for workers with large families, and so on.

Every day we can see how the media, especially television, stage, screen, publicity and the press often present the relationship between man and woman as one where the self-donation characteristic of love is substituted by a momentary possession of the other. Physical relationship is reduced to an "erotic game." And the very idea of "sin" in this field has lost all meaning.

Young people

Among young people the idea has penetrated that marriage is something that belongs to the past, and that it only makes sense for a man and a woman simply to live together. It is a relationship, therefore, that lasts as long as they feel like it, and is broken off if their feelings for one another change.

We have all seen how this provisionalness of the couple, causing insecure relationships, leads many to despair after various experiences of this kind. And the suicide rate is very high among the young.

In this context, many children find themselves without the natural support of their parents, and they grow up in a climate of uncertain and precarious relationships. This leads to desperation, to a lack of confidence in life, to psychological insecurity, to drugs, and violence.

Furthermore, this mentality leads young people, who still wish to form a stable family, to consider pre-marital relationships as normal practice.

And, in this state of decline of the family, the elderly are alienated and no longer find their rightful place.

Lastly, many women are now seeking a new identity due to their rightful need to fulfil themselves outside the family as well as within it. Their working, pursuing professions, and activity in society sometimes lead them to undervalue their roles as wives and mothers.

These are the main problems facing the family of our day. This tragic picture compelled the successors of the Apostles at the Synod of Bishops on the Family in 1980 to stress repeatedly in their final message that, because of the need for forgiveness, family members should turn frequently to the sacrament of penance.

My dear friends, this is also the picture that presents itself to us today: a truly dramatic picture from a Christian point of view. And we would spontaneously want to ask: Who is to blame?

It may be true that the world is what the family has made it, but undoubtedly the opposite holds true as well— the family is a product of society.

The world of our day is often wallowing in mud, and it is unlikely that the family, which is immersed in this world can emerge healthy. Thus the family is in dire need of the special help of grace. Our hearts certainly desire a different kind of situation, the kind of epoch in which Christian virtues would shine forth, and the family is respected, praised and imitated. But God has given us life now, and we must love *our* times. We must make every effort to render both the family and the world what they should be.

We know that in our times God has brought various Christian movements to life which support the bishops' pastoral teachings for families. Undoubtedly, each one of these Church-approved movements has its own gifts, its own charism, aimed at healing the family from a particular point of view.

The New Families Movement

And so, it comes natural to ask ourselves: Where does the New Families Movement want to begin in bringing about this healing? Which remedy does it use and what source does it draw from?

God who is Love is undoubtedly the remedy and the source, because the family is nothing other than an intertwining of relationships. It is a treasure chest, a mystery of love: nuptial love, maternal love, filial love, fraternal love, love of a grandmother for her grandchildren, the love of the children for their grandfather, for their aunts, for their cousins.... Nothing else constitutes a family, binds it together, makes it be, but love. And if the family has failed in the world, it is because love has diminished. When love dies out, the family disintegrates.

This is why our families must go to the source of love. Only God who is Love knows what the family is. He is the architect who planned it as the masterpiece of love, the sign, symbol, prototype of all the other designs. If God fashioned the family, forming it with love, then he is able to make the family sound again through love.

Created in the image of God

We know that we are being true to our nature as human beings if we behave according to what we are: persons created in the image of God. That is to say, if we remain in communion with God, if we understand our position as the "you" of God. Similarly, the love that unites a family is truly love if it remains in, is nourished and sustained by, is measured against, and communicates with the love that is in God, with that love which is the gift of God.

This is why the Church recommends frequent participation in the life of the sacraments. They bring grace and enrich us with supernatural love. She also invites families to pray together and participate in the liturgy, to nourish themselves on the Word of God, to take advantage of the traditional and contemporary devotions, particularly those associated with the Blessed Virgin which are rich sources of growth in the life of grace.

When love is enkindled and alive in the hearts of those who make up the family, impossible problems do not arise, insurmountable obstacles do not present themselves, irremediable failures do not occur. The family returns once again to being beautiful, united and healthy as God intended it to be.

A new kind of family

In our day families need a powerful dose of that love. And this is the meaning behind the title of our meeting today: *The Family and Love.*

Our Movement must lead all the families it meets to this decision: to revitalize the love that is innate in every family with that love which is a pure gift of God. In this way, Love will renew love. If this happens, since all things work together for the good of those who love (cf. Rom. 8:28), the difficulties that today afflict the family in the world, will bear fruit. A new kind of family will be born, ready to meet the needs of our times, the kind of family that the signs of the times foretell.

This love that comes from above will contribute to making those families egoistically closed in upon themselves— the kind of family that we find challenged today— more open to the world around them.

This love will be the best means for re-evaluating the role of women, giving them their true place in society.

This strong love will create an increasing awareness on the part of many men of their responsibility to take a more active part in the life of the family. It will help them to share with their wives every aspect of family life on a level of equality.

This love will strengthen all the good that, despite everything, is emerging today in the family: like a greater desire for sincerity and openness, and greater simplicity, easier communication, and fewer complexes in the relationships between boys and girls, who nowadays usually grow up together from early childhood.

True values

The love of God in everyone's heart will lead to a true re-discovery of the bodily dimension of life. No longer will it be considered maliciously, but rather seen with all its positive aspects as part of the created order.

This love will also accelerate the process already under way to reject the eroticism promoted by our culture. It will help to redimension it so as to allow the development of other interests in life— such as social, political or cultural interests.

And only the love that comes from God is able to offer a true and reliable measure for determining responsible parenthood.

In our modern world, despite all the negative elements, we are going through a period of searching and deep transformation. It is impossible to think of turning back. Anyone who has true values to propose can influence people in many ways. There are those who offer models of united families with authentic rather than oppressive relationships. There are families who are open toward the society that surrounds them, who make enlightened choices in the interests of life, and the good of their children. They heal broken relationships between generations, and rediscover the role of the elderly.

So today, my dear friends, we will speak of the family. We will deal with the family as a whole. We will take an in-depth look at the problems facing the family. We will consider parent-child relationships. We will examine the situation of orphans, of engaged couples, of widows and widowers, of the elderly, of adoption. We will confront the problem of abortion. We will look again at the vocation of our New Families Movement, its spirituality, its service to the local Church, its relationships with non-Christians and non-believers. We will listen to a wide variety of experiences. We will look at the doctrine of the Church on the family, and we will also listen to the words of the Holy Father. What else can we say?

What can we add to such an intense agenda, so complete in itself?

The model

It seems to me that if we want to give back to the family its true countenance and restore its beauty, then besides the talks, advice, guidance, and experiences that will be presented, great value will need to be given to the family of Nazareth. It is after all the luminous and universal example that eternal Wisdom has invented. All families can look to this family as a model and prototype. Not only families as such, but each member of every family can be inspired by the family of Nazareth to know what attitudes to assume, what relationships to foster, and what virtues to improve.

Every man on earth who is a husband and father will always be able to find in Joseph— Mary's husband and the foster father of Jesus— a light, a stimulus, a source of inspiration. From Joseph he will learn fidelity at all costs, heroic chastity, strength, quiet diligence, respect, veneration, protection for the mother of his children, and a participation in the family cares.

And every woman who is a wife and mother will be able to discover in Mary the person she is called to be, her equality to man, her own identity. In Mary, as Joseph's wife, she will see her own desire to share a leading role completely fulfilled. From Mary she will understand how to go beyond the family circle in order to share her rich qualities to the benefit of many: her capacity for self-sacrifice, her interior life which makes her confident, her inclination to the religious aspect of life, and her innate need to elevate herself and others on to a higher plane with her sense of innocence, beauty and purity.

In a similar way, children will find in Jesus, in his family life in Nazareth, two conflicting, and often disturbing, tendencies resolved in marvelous unity. That is, on the one hand the need to assert themselves as a generation called to open a new chapter in history and, on the other, the desire to find protection in the security of their family through love and obedience.

Yes, the Holy Family is the masterpiece of human coexistence. It mirrors the life of the Trinity where love makes God one. May this family stand before us and together with us, and may it be our guide, so that this day may be for the good of the family in the world and in the Church, and for the glory of God.

Love and the Christian Family

This talk was not given specifically to families but to the Diocese of Frascati near Rome. On 2 May 1982, Chiara Lubich was invited to address the Eucharistic Diocesan Conference in Frascati Cathedral. At first sight it might appear strange to include this talk within the context of discussion about the family. However, this is important reading for both families and the wider Church alike.

Chiara shows that the Church needs to look at the family in order to be fully itself, to live out is own real nature. On the other hand, the Christian family cannot find its true fulfilment without being nourished by all that the Church has to offer. This mutual edification is perhaps best summed up by the words of Pope John Paul II during his visit to the Familyfest in 1981 when he said spontaneously: "I wanted to say to you that I want you to become the Church. But now I say to you, may the Church become you."

The secret for this mutual enrichment is for all Christians to live as Jesus lived, which Chiara illustrates by some telling references to the Beatitudes. This will ensure that charity is alive at the heart of the Church. In turn this will allow Jesus in the eucharist to be fully effective.

The eucharist has two main consequences. It allows us as individuals to reach our full potential, which is to become another Christ. It also creates the Body of Christ, as a community. The eucharist therefore unites us to Jesus, both individually and corporately. It makes us Church and therefore family. The eucharist is fundamental to anyone who strives for the unity which Jesus asked of the Father (John 17:21).

This talk contains a powerful image: just as we eat the eucharist, so we too must allow ourselves to be devoured by our neighbour. I find the idea of being devoured a useful metaphor for family life! It also reminds me of the medieval Christian symbol of the pelican. Legend has it that the mother pelican would peck open her own breast in order to feed her young. This has become a symbol of the sacrifice of Christ and is a fitting image particularly for parents.

The Eucharist Makes Us God's Family

He is here

We are gathered here for the celebration of the Eucharistic Congress, a "moment of God" (as it has been called), having as its theme: *The eucharist makes the Church, and the Church makes the eucharist.* It is a "moment of God" lasting seven days, but to be lived one moment at a time.

I have half an hour to present some ideas that might help us see how the Congress' theme can be put into practice. I am sure that my presentation will really have its full effect if we live this brief time together as nothing more or less than a moment of God, in other words for God alone.

God is present

If we gather here in Jesus and the way he wants, which means in mutual respect and love, he— as we know— will be here in our midst: where two or more are united in his name, there he is present (cf. Matt. 18:20). And if he is with us, he will enlighten our minds, warm our hearts, spur our wills: he will place light and fire beneath every word.

So let us make clear at once exactly why we have come. It is not because this is something we enjoy, just because we like taking part in a celebration; nor is it to hear something new, we have not come here for that, nor is it out of a need to go to church, nor even to please another person. No. We are here to show God our love by this act of listening, or, as in my case, by giving this talk.

The eucharist makes the Church

"The eucharist makes the Church" is the first part of the Congress.

But what is the Church? It is the Body of Christ, the continuation of Christ. But how does the eucharist make the Church? To understand that, perhaps it would be useful to take a look at the effect of the eucharist compared with the effect of the other sacraments.

The other sacraments unite us with Christ through the particular grace of each. The sacrament of baptism, for instance, washes away original sin and all our other sins, which makes it the sacrament of rebirth. The sacrament of matrimony confers grace to live married life united in Christ.

What the eucharist does is different. It gives us Jesus himself. In the eucharist it is Jesus himself who comes into us.

It transforms us into him

And what is it that Jesus does in us? This is stupendous: he transforms us into himself. This is really extraordinary, extraordinary, but it's true, it's really true.

Saint Thomas Aquinas says: "The proper effect of the eucharist is the transformation of the human person into God":[1] his divinization. Lumen Gentium says: "The sharing in the body and blood of Christ has no other effect than to accomplish our transformation into that which we receive."[2]

It is not the same as with the food we eat at table, which gets turned into us; it is different— just the opposite: we become him, because (says Saint Albert the Great) every time that two things are joined together, the stronger prevails, the more powerful transforms the weaker into itself. Consequently, this food possessing a force more powerful than those who consume it, transforms them into itself, that is, into Jesus.[3]

The Fathers— and this is beautiful— and Doctors of the Church speak plainly: "In the form of bread his body is given you and in the form of wine his blood, to make you become, after you have partaken of Christ's body and blood, *concorporeal and consanguineous* with him."[4]

We become "bone of his bones, flesh of his flesh, members of his members."[5]

It does not bring about a physical union but a union of our persons with the glorified body of Christ present in the eucharist. We really are concorporeal, but in a sense which is new, mystical. It's a tremendous thing!

---

1. Thomas Aquinas, *Commentary on the Sentences of Peter Lombard* IV, D. 12, q. 2, a. 1.

2. "Dogmatic Constitution on the Church," 26 in *The Documents of Vatican II* (Collegeville, MN: The Liturgical Press, 1992), 381-382.

3. Cf. Thomas Aquinas, *Sentences* IV, 9, 2-B 29, 217.

4. Cyril and John of Jerusalem, *Mystical Catechesis* 4, 3 in J.P. Migne, *Patrologia Graeca* 33, 1100.

5. Albert the Great, *De Euch.* 3, 1, 5-B 38, 257.

Productive of unity

The eucharist does not just produce a transformation of each individual Christian into Christ, but as a real sacrament of unity it produces unity between people too, communion between brothers and sisters, brothers and sisters in Jesus and brothers and sisters to each other; it forms the family of God's children.

By means of the eucharist Jesus unites Christians to himself, and among themselves, in a single body. This is how he gives life to the church in its innermost substance, where it is nothing but charity, unity, body of Christ.

Truly the eucharist makes the Church. This is the marvel it brings about.

Conditions

Naturally we all know of course that for the eucharist to have its proper effects it needs certain conditions. We learned this in catechism.

It is logical that when we receive communion we cannot receive those effects and those fruits if we do not, for example, believe in what Jesus teaches, if we don't desire to put his commands into practice, if we don't go to confession beforehand, if we do not leave our gift at the altar and go to be reconciled with our brothers first, and then come back (in case something needs to be put straight), and so forth. There are a lot of conditions, we know what they are; we have seen them, and are familiar with them from catechism.

Similar to Jesus

If it is only on certain conditions that the eucharist produces all these effects (our transformation into Jesus and of all of us into a single body, the Church) and only on certain conditions that those effects will last, a definite kind of conduct is required.

Into what does the eucharist transform us? Into Christ. And what then do we become? We become Jesus. And how must we then behave? Obviously, as he did. Jesus can only live like Jesus. His feelings, his way of thinking, his way of seeing things have to become our own, his way of acting must be ours.

Blessed are those who suffer

For example, Jesus calls "blessed" those who suffer affliction, those who weep. Jesus thinks that human pain, if it is joined well to his, is a fountain of joy even already on this earth and, of course, is a guarantee of joy to come. Is that how Jesus thinks? Then even if the world around us does not think that way at all, we Christians have to, otherwise this effect does not last.

In this world that we know so well, the world which often pursues happiness at all costs in hedonism and drugs, we Christians have to show that even in tears you can be happy. Everything that others call hard luck, misfortune, can all become, in the perspective of Christ, a motive for pure and profound joy, productive of good.

Blessed are the poor

Jesus also calls "blessed" the poor in spirit, which means those who are detached from the things of earth, and he adds, "because theirs is the kingdom of heaven" (Matt. 5:3). We have to say the same.

In a world like ours where consumerism pervades everything like foul air, where materialism freezes our hearts in the bitterly impatient desire for well-being that is only earthly, in a world like this we have to swim against the current and keep our hearts completely detached.

Blessed are the pure

Jesus is also convinced that the pure of heart are "blessed." Purity: who speaks of purity today? There is no talk of purity, no one wants to speak of purity anymore, it's a forgotten word.

Why? Because it stings us. It hurts. So let it hurt— we have to be consistent. The pain does not exempt us from living it deeply and completely. For example, the life of Jesus within us, brought by way of the eucharist, is irreconcilable with how so easily these days we watch just any television show that is on. It is irreconcilable with the reading of certain newspapers, with the seeing of certain films, with the display of certain kinds of clothing. The two just do not go together. We have to go against the tide.

Christians are called to see God: "Blessed are the pure because they shall see God" (Matt. 5:8); that is their amazing future. Those who have set themselves a goal to attain do not limit their efforts, they are not afraid of training for it. Neither should Christians limit themselves in the pains that purity can cost them.

Blessed are the peacemakers

Again, Jesus says: "Blessed are the peacemakers" (Matt. 5:9). With today's tensions between East and West, between races, and in some countries between rich and poor, in the midst of wars and terrorism, and all such things, we have to be bringers of peace. Where do we start from? From ourselves, in ourselves.

When we get bothered about something, we have to make peace in ourselves. We don't know where it may lead to otherwise. For if we let that something inside us explode, we become a source of tension. Next we must bring peace to our families, to our workplace, to our schools. It is impossible to measure the effect of this way of acting. We don't know the extent of the good it will do: it is like tossing a stone into water. While on the other hand, who knows what might have happened if we had not actually behaved as peacemakers?

Blessed are the merciful

Next Jesus wishes for mercy: "Blessed are the merciful" (Matt. 5:7). We know what Jesus demands (and here we could review the whole Gospel point by point); we know that we cannot keep up our transformation in Christ, we cannot keep up our being the living Church, if we do not live all his words.

Somebody could interrupt and object that it is hard. He said so many things! How can we possibly keep them all in mind? Even then . . . they are so difficult! But you can't deny it: Jesus did not come just by chance and his teaching is not something merely to be played with. It is difficult, and his words are many. Nevertheless there is one word, a single word that sums them all up: love, love of God, love of those around us.

A way to begin

The Scriptures say, and the saints confirm it, that in love one finds all the virtues. Not only that, but when one loves (you have only to try it), everything becomes easy. One of the Psalms says: "I run the way of your commandments, for you enlarge my understanding" (119:32). That is truly the way it is: one runs, it is easy to carry out what Jesus says, when love is in one's heart.

So we have a thing to begin with, something we can commit ourselves to, in order to put something into practice, so that this congress will have really been helpful: begin to love. Have a try, try it. Then this "something," our transformation in Christ which the eucharist effects, will last.

But then we have also seen that the eucharist does not only transform us in Christ, but it also makes us one as brothers and sisters to each other, making us into God's family. And so that this family of God, this way of actually being Church, may last, we too must play our part. We cannot get something for nothing. No indeed, we must do our part.

And so, as our way to begin: if we love we will have every virtue, because love is like a summary of them all. All the other virtues help, but love sums them all up.

Working together

But something has to be done, to make permanent our actually being the Church, our being a body, our being a family, God's family—just as we here are a little like this, like God's family.

Every family, you are well aware, has certain requirements; even natural families have their laws. Take, for example, one characteristic of a natural family, of a good family, even though such families are few in this world, which is that everyone lives together. Its members: father, mother, children, grandparents, all live under the same roof.

Then there are certain moments when the communal nature of a family's life stands out clearly, for example, when they are all sitting together at table. Whereas in every family each member has some small personal possessions, a toy or something, nevertheless generally speaking, everything is held in common. Whatever one person in the family may be suffering is felt by all. Each is worried, helps, or saves for the other. There could be one who gives up his or her nights to care for another who is sick, or who takes on more work to make up for another's inadequate salary.

And the joy of one is the joy of all: they feel glad at another's promotion or at weddings, they celebrate birthdays, these things are joys for everyone in the family.

It is still true today that the wise lessons given by parents in good families are handed down as rules of life.

In every family that is the way God made it to be, there is solidarity, mutual love, understanding, and sharing.

The first Christian communities

The family of all God's children also has its own characteristics. But is there an example we Christians of the twentieth century can follow, a model of how this family could be for it to be as close as possible to the idea God has for it, the family of God's children?

I do not think we can find a better model than the first Christian communities. There are four distinctive elements by which they stand out: mutual love, common ownership of goods, prayer, particularly the breaking of bread around the eucharistic table, and listening to the word of the apostles.

The call to us Christians today is to reactivate this experience once more, in every form of corporate life, in our ecclesial communities, in our parishes, and in our dioceses.

The one root

This too is hard, it is hard to carry out all four elements. How can it be done? Or better, what is the root, the one root from which grow those four principal elements typical of the first Christian communities?

The life of a natural family expresses itself in various ways— I've mentioned some already. They are all the result of mutual love binding its members together and becoming the soul and cement of the family. It's the same for the family of God's children.

Mutual love is the secret, that is where the secret lies, in love. Love always is the secret of Christian life.

How is it done?

To whom do we look to know how to love?

If the eucharist's job is to make us become concorporeal— as we have said— and consanguineous with Christ, to make us the Church, it is also the model of how Christians should behave in order to love. Let me explain. How does one go about loving? The eucharist teaches us.

As many of you know, I have had to travel a lot around the world. I have found myself on different continents, among different language groups, and different peoples. You feel it, when you are a long way from home. You feel it. Well, it makes quite an impression, in the midst of the world of perhaps a totally different religion, to enter a little Christian, Catholic church and see that exactly the same Jesus as ours is there in the eucharist, the same as in our own Cathedral, as in Saint Peter's: all of him is there for all people, all of him for each person. It makes an impression!

There you understand one thing at least about loving. If Jesus gives his whole self to all, we too must love all. We are called to universal brotherhood. All are candidates for his Mystical Body, all are destined (or it should be their destiny, they just have to find it) to be Christ's followers, everyone is made for him.

That is his first lesson. Truly, Jesus has no preferences for people, he does not discriminate.

Let oneself be eaten

In the eucharist Jesus teaches us also the way to approach people.

What is the meaning of love? Does not loving mean

making ourselves one with everybody? Making ourselves one in everything they want, in the smallest and most insignificant things and in those that may not mean much to us, but that might mean a lot to them?

And Jesus has given a stupendous example of what this way of acting means, precisely by instituting the eucharist. There he makes himself bread in order to enter into everyone, to make himself edible, to make himself one with each and every one, to be of service, to love everyone.

Therefore let us too make ourselves one, to the point of letting ourselves be eaten up. This is the meaning of love, making ourselves one, so that others feel nourished by our love, comforted, lifted up, understood. A mother, for example, is not in the least ashamed to make herself one with her baby, till she almost makes people think she is no longer capable of normal speech, because of her baby-talk. It is love which drives her to do this. She makes herself one with the baby and it laughs. A father plays with his little boy and he is not ashamed to be seen playing with him, wasting his time, playing cards or some other game; he is not ashamed, and it is fun for the child. And a fiancé might think up all kinds of things for his loved one, and thus love grows.

Making oneself one

Those who love make themselves truly one. And if our duty at some point may be to give correction, in this kind of atmosphere our correction would even be accepted. Let's make ourselves one in everything, everything, as Jesus who became human in everything except sin.

Imitate Jesus who, though God, became human like

one of us. He worked like us, lived in a family like us, and he spent time sleeping and resting like us. He did all this to be like us, he even ate as we do: he made himself one in everything, except in sin. As it is said today, Jesus truly "lived the other." He became human, God became human and really "lived the other."

And so, if others weep, weep with them. If they laugh, laugh with them, be glad at things with them, rejoice to see them nourished by our love. Do everything, everything, but just for love, without any self-interest, otherwise it is no longer love.

Make ourselves one even with non-believers, discover and understand the positive needs which are always present in them, share their ideals too, as far as possible.

This "making ourselves one" is above all an almost infallible apostolic method. Paul says so: "To the weak I became weak, so that I might win the weak. I have become all things to all people, that I might by all means save some" (1 Cor. 9:22).

It gets results if we do it disinterestedly. They may not come immediately, they may come years later, but they will come, we must be sure of it. The day will come, today or tomorrow, when our brother or sister, touched by our "making ourselves one," our way of loving, will share our Christian convictions.

This "making ourselves one" naturally brings about mutual love among Christians, like us here now in this church, desirous one and all that Jesus in the eucharist may have a maximum effect in our hearts. And mutual love is the necessary condition for the permanence of the eucharist's effect, which is to make us Church.

Mutual love

Mutual love between Christians! We have no idea how important it is to make it a reality today. If we come to each other's aid in a practical way, materially and spiritually, if our journey to God is made together, seeking our own perfection as well as others', if we are ready to die for one another as Jesus wants, then we will have performed for our times the most useful, most proper, and most eagerly awaited service.

If there is anything to which the world today is most sensitive (and Paul VI has said this), it is deeds, deeds. In our times, people do not listen to lecturers so much as to witnesses, to people who have done something.[6]

We also know that one of Jesus' promises stands behind the fulfilment of this: if we are one, the world will believe.

They had seen

I had occasion a few months ago to proclaim the message of Jesus to twelve thousand Buddhists in Japan They wanted to know about my experience in contact with Jesus. I was able to verify what a great contribution Christians can make to the Kingdom of God if they *live* their faith. It is a great contribution!

These Buddhist leaders had already known groups of Christians— belonging to our Focolare Movement— in various parts of the world. For that reason, they believed what I said. My words even touched on the mysteries of

---

6. Cf. Pope Paul VI, General Audience, 10 February 1974.

faith, difficult subjects therefore, like the Trinity; but they had a profound reception, because these people had seen Christians who loved one another.

And I had the feeling that I was satisfying something, satisfying an infinite hunger. I had the feeling that the world which does not know Christ is looking for nothing else but him and his word. But we have first to give witness, show life. We have to live up to the eucharist, let it truly bring about the Church in us.

Rebuild

I have the impression, as I travel the world, that in many countries, and certain countries in particular, Christians find themselves in the same situation as Saint Francis when our Lord invited him to rebuild the Church.

Nowadays, in the secularism that dampens religious spirit, and in the various winds of materialism that freeze it, the Church is at times in need of rebuilding, at times almost of being refounded. But, though the Church is not in this condition everywhere (in our diocese it is certainly not), it is nevertheless everywhere in need of some repairs: a window somewhere, here a pillar, there a doorway, or the floor. . . .

From our local Church too, and for our local Church, our diocese, undoubtedly God is expecting something.

And look! The Eucharistic Congress has come, to bring an extraordinary message, the secret of who is capable of building or rebuilding the Church. Just so: the eucharist makes the Church. And it makes it with our co-operation, with our love.

Come and see

My dear Christians, the local Church of which we form part is a bit special. It is close to Rome where people come from all over the world, looking for Christianity.

It also houses the international headquarters of movements, to which people converge from every nation of Europe and beyond.

What do you think? Would it not be an excellent fruit of this Eucharistic Congress if we were, first of all, to make a decision to nourish ourselves as often as possible on the body of our Lord; and next, with his aid, we were to launch ourselves upon this divine adventure of loving, loving, loving with our whole heart?

Loving, and loving one another, so that the eucharist we receive may have its full effect. This is the way we can increase the beauty of our Church, renovate it and even make it live where it never was alive before.

Would it not be wonderful to raise up, here close to Rome and to the Pope, a local Church so alive that we could say to many: "come and see"? It might seem just a dream, but it can become reality.

May our Lady, model and type of the Church, hold this dream in her heart. And may she who is so loved here in Frascati, if she thinks, and if she wants, use even us to make it happen. She will also tell us what she thinks through our bishop and our priests, who among other things have the power to make the eucharist, so that the eucharist may make the Church.

Love Is the Origin of Life

The setting for this talk was the Sports Stadium in Florence, Italy on 17 May 1986, when fifteen thousand people gathered for a congress organized by the Pro-Life Movement of Florence. Chiara, together with Mother Teresa of Calcutta, was among the guest speakers at this event.

Chiara's talk is not so much an anti-abortion rally cry, but an affirmation of life. As such, while there are things that people from other religious traditions or other Churches might express differently, or even details they might occasionally disagree with, her essential message has something to say to everyone. As she develops her theme, Chiara traces the theological reasons from the Old to the New Testament, and from the Fathers of the Church, that demonstrate why the universal Christian tradition is always to affirm the sanctity of life.

Every life calls for love— not just the unborn child but all human life. This includes the adolescent coming to terms with their own sexuality; the single mother who needs the support of the community rather than its condemnation; people who are sick, handicapped or elderly. In Eastern cultures, for instance, older people are respected for their experience and their wisdom. The West needs to re-examine its attitude to its senior citizens who are so often regarded merely as unproductive units in our consumer society.

This talk is not just a critique of the ills of society, but a profound explanation of life and human fulfilment. Chiara is not afraid to raise all the issues which surround this emotive and complex area. Love is defined thus: "To give true love to one another means to give God (divine love) to one another" as supernatural love purifies, fortifies and makes human love everlasting. Sexuality too is placed within the context of this love: a love which reflects the total gift of self by Christ on the cross. Suffering, seen in the same light of the cross, is not something that is necessarily negative and to be avoided at all costs, but is at the heart of the Christian experience of love.

During this meeting Chiara Lubich and Mother Teresa signed a joint "Appeal to Europe" which was sent to various European Economic Community institutions and to the leaders of the European Community. Here is a brief extract from that appeal: "Just as Christian Florence was the cradle of humanism and the renaissance, so too may Europe whose roots are Christian, be the heart of a new renaissance, animated by a sense of ethics which values the human person: glory of the living God, and of the highest order of creation. May the first stone of the edifice of peace be respect for human life, particularly that which is newly born, suffering and dying."

Every Life Calls for Love

We are gathered here today to celebrate life. Is it necessary to speak of life in our times? Yes, it certainly is. Unfortunately, in many parts of the world, what we could call a civilization of death prevails: abortion slaughters the lives of the innocent; sterilization, genetic manipulation, and euthanasia are commonplace; there is no stopping rearmament, and meanwhile wars carry on; people talk about bringing back capital punishment; there is the constant threat of terrorism, and a succession of murders, suicides, drug-related violence.

Technological and scientific progress, furthermore, generates near panic in the face of life. In fact, such progress does not only bring about the hope of better conditions for humanity, it also brings about increasing anxiety for the future. An anti-life mentality is spreading due to the prospect of a nuclear war, the exaggerated fear of over-population, the excessive concern for material goods and the rejection of spiritual riches, and the view of procreation as something negative, even to be feared.

Yet life is a subject about which all people of faith and of the most diverse ideologies should be in agreement. But this is not always the case. There are so many ideas and there is such a variety of opinions concerning the value of life and its complex problems, that the different opinions condition even people with the best of intentions.

God's idea of life

Consequently, we come to desire to see and to understand what God thinks. For those of us who have faith, his idea on such an important question is a determining factor. Since we have all been created in the image of God and are Christian by nature, his idea cannot leave anyone indifferent— not even those who do not believe or who hold different beliefs. This is true especially for those who are pure, sincere and genuine.

Let us confidently examine God's idea. God's idea! How can we even understand, or at least have an intuition of it? In the first place, we can understand it by reading the sacred texts, which open up as a hymn to life. God calls the whole universe into being, giving life to plants, animals, and finally to man and woman, who are created in his own "image and likeness."

But God does not only bring the universe into existence. He also wants to sustain it by establishing laws, by giving it an order to be followed. He wants to assure life to all living creatures by feeding them the proper food and by telling each species to multiply so that they may fill the earth.

Following Adam and Eve's grave disobedience, God tells the woman: ". . . in pain shall you bring forth children" (Gen. 3:16), and says to the man: ". . . by the sweat of your face you shall eat bread," and "to dust you shall return" (Gen. 3:19). Even though he punishes them in terms of these vital aspects of their existence, God still manifests himself as the God of life. The story of Genesis, in fact, does not end with punishment, but with the announcement of salvation.

There is always this respect for life in the Old Testament. For example, even when God must punish, indeed destroy, in the story of the flood, he saves Noah. And as he did with Adam, he gives this new founder of humanity the same blessing and the same affirmation: ". . . from human beings, each one for the blood of another, I will require a reckoning of human life . . . for in his own image God made humankind" (Gen. 9:5-6).

For the first people of the Old Testament, life was considered unquestionably to be the greatest gift. A long life was the promise given to those who observed God's commands. "Honor your father and mother, as the Lord your God commanded you, so that your days may be long and that it may go well with you in the land the Lord your God is giving you" (Deut. 5:16).

The greatest good

It was a common conviction that the prolonging of physical life to "old age," when a person could finally die "full of days," was considered to be a gesture of particular divine benevolence. Yes, because the blessing of the Lord consisted in giving life. The Book of Wisdom affirms: "God did not make death, and he does not delight in the death of the living. For he created all things that they might exist" (Wisd. 1:13-14a).

Thus, in this lies the essential message of the Old Testament with regard to human life: the human person, the whole of the human person has been created in the image of God; not only the spirit (as we would say today), but also the body is a reflection of this image. Thus, whoever injures another person's body, injures the image of God.

And an important consequence of the divine origin of life, of the fact that the human person has been created by God in his own image, is that the human person cannot dispose of himself or herself as he or she wills. God is the Lord of life. Consequently, human beings possess their life as something that is loaned to them. In this regard, the Old Testament draws the conclusion in one of the Ten Commandments: "You shall not murder" (Deut. 5:17).

The source of life

The New Testament is likewise an exaltation of life. In the Book of Revelation Jesus is called, "The living one": "I am the first and the last, and the living one" (Rev. 1:17-18). And the same attribute is given to God: ". . . You are the Christ, the Son of the living God" (Matt. 16:16).

The whole mission of Jesus is to give both supernatural and natural life. He says of himself: "I am the resurrection and the life" (John 11:25). And he says: "I am the way, the truth, and the life" (John 14:6). Jesus demonstrated his love for life very clearly by raising the dead and healing every kind of illness. The Good News does not end with the death on the cross, but with the resurrection.

The early Christians were still imbued with the teaching of Jesus, who not too long before had been on earth. They applied his commandments, which were in the interest of life, to every aspect and every moment of human existence. In the *Didache*, the important first century manual of Christian instruction, we read that "among the many sins of those who follow the way of death is that they kill their children and with abortion they are destroyers of God's image."[7]

And Tertullian, who lived between the second and third centuries, expressed his point of view very clearly when he said: "For us Christians murder is forbidden once and for all. We are not permitted to destroy even the conceived creature in the womb."[8]

All the Greek and Latin Fathers of the Church considered the unborn child as sacred, because it is willed by God. This child must be protected. Thus for a Christian, even life conceived out of wedlock comes from God and is entitled to develop freely.

This is a brief outline of God's idea on the sacredness of life— which is not to be tampered with— as it emerges from the Sacred Scripture and from the doctrine of the Church Fathers.

The call to defend life

The best qualified interpreters of God's will throughout the centuries— also on this subject— are the popes and bishops, who are successors of the Apostles. Jesus was referring to them when he said: "Whoever listens to you listens to me" (Luke 10:16). Thus Jesus speaks through them. We all know how the Holy Father, John

---

7. *Didache*, V. 2. See also *The Letter of Barnabas,* from the second century: "Do not murder the child with abortion, do not take its life as soon as it is born"; and also from the second century, Athenagoras of Athens in his writing, *What Is Required of Christians*, 35, 6: "Those who employ certain means for abortion are committing murder and will be held accountable for this in front of God."

8. Tertullian, *Apologeticum*, 9, 8.

Paul II, values life. His heart, like that of the bishops, throbs in a special way for these very serious problems. And he often zealously defends the many lives which may be suppressed. He recently affirmed: "The modern social context seems to call for a particularly decisive effort on the part of every person of good will *to defend life,* from its first blossoming in the maternal womb to the final moments of its inevitable decline."[9]

Motherhood

This then is God's idea: do not kill, do not ever kill!

It is a fact that the child to be born is a human being from the moment of conception. The child, therefore, is not an extension of the mother: he or she is another human being. Children are not their mother's property. There are no rights over them once they have come into being. On the contrary, there is the basic duty to do everything possible to protect their life. A woman's greatness, her personal growth lies in being the cause of life, not in suppressing the child of her womb.

Motherhood, however, does not always come with joy and hope in the heart of mothers. At times motherhood costs. It costs suffering and sacrifice. To give birth to children, to raise, maintain and educate them entails anxieties, worries . . . sleepless nights, disappointments, money. Sometimes the act of generation is not an act of love, but the result of a man's violence of a woman, outside and inside of matrimony. Sometimes uncomfortable economic situations make it more difficult to accept

---

9. John Paul II, "To Clergy and Pastors," 12 May, 1985 in *La Traccia,* vol. 5, p. 530.

the new baby. Sometimes the precarious physical condition of the woman can weigh heavily on the decision to have a child. The woman who works outside the home and at the same time looks after the house, feels an oppressive burden that lessens her enthusiasm to have children. Sometimes the child comes as the consequence of immature relationships between two partners unprepared to receive the child. Frequently, due to the lack of understanding around her, influenced by consumerism and physical comfort, the woman experiences a painful loneliness in resisting the temptation of abortion.

God relies on love

Yet God repeats: "Do not kill, do not kill." But God is not a tyrant. He is so demanding because he has provided even in difficult circumstances the way, and has given the means to help carry out this commandment. How? God relies on the love living in human hearts and has strengthened it in a divine way. He has engrafted on this love the love that comes from on high, and has enkindled in human hearts the flame of divine love.

It is always an amazing spectacle to see how in springtime the warmth of the sun can transform nature. Everything comes to life and buds forth. Trees turn green and are bedecked with blossoms.

It is something wonderful to see that even during the winter, the earth was guarding and protecting the seeds which now throb with life. But it takes the warmth of the sun to make them blossom.

It is not spring as we find it marked on the calendar, not 21 March, that works this explosion of life. It is the sun with its warmth that causes it. If it gets warm early, even if it is still wintertime, the earth does not ask whether or not spring has come. It blossoms anyway.

The essence of the gospel

And just as the sun makes life blossom in nature, only love in the hearts of human beings can bring about the triumph of life.

Today, as we said earlier, there is a civilization of death. A strong current of Christian love pervading our entire society would be the best prevention against these evils of our time and would give us the strength to do everything possible to eliminate or diminish them.

Love is the essence of the Gospel; it is the specific vocation of the followers of Christ. Thus we must renew divine love in hearts: the divine love which Jesus brought to the world and wishes to see enkindled.

We receive this gift with baptism. If we partake of the other sacraments, if we practise the virtues taught by Christ, if we pray, this love will remain with us, it will be nourished, it will grow, and it will make the "yoke" of motherhood light and gentle.

This was the experience of the early Christians. For this reason they obeyed what Jesus, and later the Apostles, and later still the Church Fathers, said. And they did it with joy. If today's mothers have this love in their hearts, they will see no difficulty in giving life to the children that God sends them. They will courageously face even the most difficult situations.

Responsible fathers

And if love is kept alive in the hearts of Christians, it will also not be hard to ask men to accept their share of responsibility. Children in fact do not belong to the mother alone, but to both parents.

Nowadays there is a tendency to portray motherhood as a subject concerning only women. But it is not so. In the best way, love will bring about in the hearts of men the sense of responsibility toward the lives which they too have generated. If we lose sight of this common responsibility, we destroy the very meaning of the family seen as a community of two people united in love, looking forward to new life. Another consequence would be a tendency to separate humanity into two parts: the woman and the child on one side, and the man, selfish and indifferent, on the other.

Furthermore, love for God and love for those around us are nourished one by the other. As when the deeper a plant thrusts down its roots, the higher it shoots toward the sky, so the more a Christian loves others, the more profound is his or her union with God. And in this union with God, the Christian finds a renewed need for prayer. And with this, there springs up an attraction to continence.

Charity, love, is the queen and the mother of all the virtues. It gives birth to purity and chastity, and it extinguishes all selfishness. The man who loves masters his passions, has respect for others and, therefore, also for his wife and the new human being who might come to life in her womb. When love is like this, it is possible to put into practice responsible parenthood effectively and in the right way.

Human beings need love

It is not enough, however, to love only the expected child. Human beings need love at every stage of their life and in every situation. Thus, also every child that is born needs love. Even though the child is the focus of attention, in an atmosphere of love, he or she acquires an active openness to communion which is the foundation for proper relationships with others.

When a child grows up, we have an adolescent who also needs love. As we know, the rapid process of sexual maturation which is characteristic of young people in adolescence brings them face to face with new things. They become aware of their bodies; they experience impulses of affection never experienced before; they feel a new interest in the opposite sex. This is a difficult moment. Young people can find themselves in dangerous situations. Many environments offer irresponsible freedom and a false idea of sexuality seen merely as a source of pleasure.

While the adolescent may feel that this moment in life is the beginning of a certain personal independence, it is also true that it is the moment in which his or her need of love, although hidden, is very strong. Love is needed here on the part of the parents and of all those who relate to the child in order to understand the difficult moment he or she is going through. It is necessary, with great tact, to enable a dialogue, even though it may have become difficult. Like this it is possible to hold on to the positive features of this phase of development.

And if in many of these situations parents experience moments of great concern and suffering— almost as if they were still giving birth to their child— it will be their love "soaked" in suffering that will influence the child. It will remind him or her of the greatness of giving oneself to others, of the value of sacrifice, and of respect for companions at school or at work.

Engaged couples, too, need love. A married couple

works together with the Creator in bringing new human lives into the world. Therefore, the engaged couple must learn to cultivate the nourishment of this life: Love. "To give true love to one another," said Igino Giordani, "means to give God (divine love) to one another,"[10] because supernatural love purifies, fortifies and makes human love everlasting.

Love in the face of suffering

But life is not always as it should be. People are free and at times they seriously abuse their power to choose, to the detriment of others. People can find themselves faced with painful situations: an undesired child, or an illegitimate child, or perhaps even a child that is the result of violence, or an abandoned child. The suffering of the innocent is one of the greatest mysteries of life. What answer does love give? Jesus who died and rose for every person can give us "new eyes" to recognize the immense value of every life, even in these cases.

In a family or in a community that has blossomed from Christian love, room can also be found for the mother who carries her pregnancy alone and who finds herself in serious difficulty because she is rejected by her family. It is often the timely availability of another family or of a community that helps many mothers say "yes" to life when they find themselves gripped by doubt and anguish with no prospects for the future.

The way that families can give their typical and irre-

---

10. Igino Giordani, *The Family Community of Love* (New York: New City Press, 1988).

placeable contribution is by taking in abandoned children either through adoption or guardianship. Abandoned children, even the very young, almost always have a past that is interwoven with sufferings and traumas. And the dominating note of their personality is the lack of affection. In these cases love is the first and only medicine. A child that is loved is able to overcome his or her difficulties and recover fully, can achieve the human fulfilment worthy of a son or daughter of God.

Life must be respected

There can be many other difficult situations throughout life. Life must be respected in all of these moments. If at the basis of laws or social initiatives we place a mentality of disrespect for people who are suffering, handicapped or elderly, then little by little we create a false society. We give importance only to a few values like physical well-being, strength, exaggerated productivity and power, and we distort the purpose for which a nation lives; that is, for the good of the human person and society.

Health, as we know, is a precious gift which should be protected. Thus we should do all we can so that our own bodies and those of our brothers and sisters receive nourishment and rest, and are not exposed to sicknesses, to accidents or to an exaggerated amount of sports. In fact, the body is also important for Christians. If for Jesus in the eucharist, age upon age has built splendid cathedrals that defy time, then for God who lives in a person in grace, we must care for the body which is God's temple.

But, should we lose our health, we must remember that there is a life that is not conditioned by the state of our health, but by the supernatural love that burns in our heart. And it is this superior life that gives value to our physical life even when we are sick.

The value of illness

If we consider illnesses merely from a human point of view, we can only affirm that they are misfortunes. But, if we look at these from a Christian point of view, we can see that they are trials in which we must train ourselves for the great trial that awaits all of us, when we will come face to face with the passageway to the other life.

Did not the Holy Father just recently say that illnesses are spiritual exercises that God himself gives to us? People who are sick have an added richness, another kind of richness. In speaking of asceticism and mysticism, the Church refers to illnesses not only as belonging to the field of medicine, but as purifications that God sends, therefore as small steps toward union with God. In addition, our faith tells us that when a person is sick, he or she participates in the sufferings of Christ. In this light, the sick person is another Christ crucified who can offer his or her suffering for what is of the most value, the eternal salvation of all people.

In the frenzy of work and daily life we are tempted at times to see people who suffer only as marginal cases to help so that they can quickly recover and return to their activities. It does not occur to us that they are the ones who even now can contribute the most. If people who are ill are understood and loved, they can positively carry out their role for the benefit of humanity. Love can help them to give meaning to their condition and to be aware of what they represent.

And what holds true for the sick, holds true also for the handicapped. People with a handicap need love. They need to be recognized for the value that their life has: it is sacred, as all life is sacred, with all the consequent dignity which that brings. They need to be considered as persons, and as much as possible, they should live in normal situations with other people.

A third season in life

What should we say about the elderly? Every life calls for love, and the elderly are no exception. Because of our present day's prolonged average life expectancy, the growing number of elderly even seems to be a problem. Thus, it is possible to sense a tendency in society to alienate or isolate the elderly. They are considered a social burden because they are unproductive. We speak of the elderly as being a category apart, almost as if we were not speaking of men and women.

Moreover, besides physical decline the elderly often experience a serious psychological discomfort: that of regarding oneself as a "has-been." We must give new hope to the elderly. Becoming a senior citizen is nothing other than experiencing the third season of life. The life that is born, that develops, and that declines displays three aspects of the one mystery of all life whose origin is God-Love.

In certain Asian and African countries, the elderly are highly respected because they are viewed as wise experts in life. In fact, the elderly person makes clear what is essential, what is most important. They say that when Saint John the Evangelist was in his eighties he would visit the Christian communities where they would ask him about the message of Jesus. He always replied: "Love one another," as if he had nothing more to add, because with this expression he had truly grasped the core of Christ's thought.

To deprive ourselves of the elderly is to deprive ourselves of our heritage. We must esteem and respect them by loving them. And we must esteem and respect them also when they are seriously ill, when, humanly speaking, there is no more hope, and their need for help is more demanding.

In the eyes of God, there is no such thing as a life, or a period of life, that is not worthy of being lived. Since this life is a preparation for the next that will never end, we cannot know what God wants from them even in the very last moments of their existence. For us, therefore, euthanasia is a very serious absurdity.

Civilization of life

We must love then. We must love, love, and love, because life, every life and every stage of life, calls for love. We must oppose the civilization of death with a civilization of life. Yes, today the world which is often dejected because it fears life and distressed because it suppresses life, needs love. It urgently needs an invasion of love: among the members of our families; among families; among the members of lay and religious associations; among the various movements and associations; among all Christians; among those who believe in God and all people of good will; among people everywhere, in offices, hospitals, schools and factories; among little children, young people and adults.

When God came on earth he brought love. God, the

creator of life and the cause of a new life which is even more important, knew what was needed to maintain it: love was needed. And at the end of our lives, God will judge us exclusively on love. Therefore, love is important.

Let us leave this stadium having made the resolution that our lives should be one continuous act of love toward every person we meet. Let us communicate this ardent desire to as many people as possible. In this way, we will give our contribution to that civilization which today is often spoken of: the civilization of love.

Mutual Love
Is the Best Educator

This talk was given during a conference on the topic of "The Family and Education." The word education is used here in its widest meaning: not merely education in the formal sense of learning or instruction, but in the fuller sense of "the general upbringing" of children.

The subject of "education within the family" is fundamental in a society where we often witness a general abdication of many of the responsibilities of parenthood. Chiara not only reasserts the responsibility of parents in the whole educational process of their children, but introduces some radical ideas about how to be successful educators.

She begins by stating the premise that in reality there is only one teacher: Jesus. She then goes on to outline the variety of ways in which Jesus taught his disciples— not just in word, but also through his example. The only way parents can be authentic teachers therefore is for them to become another Jesus, that is to allow Jesus, the teacher par excellence, to live in them, not just as individuals, but also through their mutual love, which then allows Jesus to live in the midst of the family. "Where two or more are gathered together in my name, there I am in their midst" (Matt. 18:20).

There is also the recognition that education within the family is not just a one-way process. Our children have something to teach us parents too. Children are quite capable of living mutual love so as to invite the presence of Christ into their midst or into the midst of the family. I have heard many people tell of how it was the children who brought about a renewal of relationships within the family— even bringing separated parents back together.

There are some strong words here as well; I was present at this meeting and vividly recall the gasp that arose in the hall when Chiara said: "Admonishment should be given with peace, calm and detachment." True, but difficult. And yet this is not only the best but perhaps the only way for the correction of a child to produce genuine and lasting fruit for both the child who is corrected and for the parent who corrects.

I think every parent will find something challenging and inspiring in this talk. It is a real vision of what our families can be like when we strive to put mutual love at their heart.

The One and Only Teacher

My dear friends, I would like to begin by greeting all of you, especially those who have come from the farthest corners of the world.

The congress arranged by the New Families Movement is beginning today. The theme of the congress is: *The family and education*. My brief talk is intended simply as an introduction to this important subject.

This congress will examine the topic in-depth, from different points of view. I would like to lay the foundation for all that will be said. If this foundation is lived out, I believe that everything will acquire more value and true value.

Speaking of education, it is logical that we find before us two subjects: the educator or teacher who must teach, and the disciple or pupil who must be taught.

Jesus the teacher

With regard to the teacher, there is a sentence from the gospel which makes us think and which can shed light on the education that should be imparted in the family.

The sentence is: "For you have one teacher, and you

are all brothers" (Matt. 23:8). Jesus recognizes one teacher alone, he himself. This does not mean that he denies the presence of authority or paternity, but that it must be interpreted not as dominion or power, but as service. For in service, which is love, it is not only the human person who acts, but Christ himself in that person. In this way, Christ continues to be the first teacher.

Jesus' example

But what kind of teacher is Jesus? In Jesus, the teacher, we can see various important characteristics. First of all, he gives an example. He himself incarnates his doctrine. He does not impose burdens before carrying them himself: "Woe to you . . ." he says. "For you load people with burdens hard to bear, and you yourselves do not lift a finger to ease them" (Luke 11:46). Jesus puts into practice what he asks of others.

Looking at him, we can deduce that the first way to educate, and this applies to parents as well, is not so much instructing or correcting, but living, with total commitment, one's own life as a Christian. Parents themselves must put into practice what they ask of their children. Do they ask for sincerity, commitment, loyalty, obedience, charity toward others, chastity, patience and forgiveness? Children should find these qualities, first of all, in their parents. Children should always be able to find in their mothers and fathers indisputable models to which they can relate.

Another characteristic of Jesus' way of educating others is to give them real, practical help, as he did when he calmed the storm on the lake (cf. Luke 8:24). On a natural level, parents do everything they possibly can for their children. But they will be able to do even more, and above all do it much better, if they root their natural love in a supernatural love; that is, if they love with God's charity, with the charity of one who takes the initiative in loving, without expecting anything in return. This is a love that never leaves others indifferent.

Free and responsible

Moreover, Jesus gives trust to those he teaches, as we can conclude from his words to the adulteress: "Go your way, and from now on do not sin again" (cf. John 8:11). He believes in the possibility of this woman beginning a life that is morally correct.

The words of parents must always be words of encouragement. They must be words charged with hope, positive words that express all their confidence in the new beginning of their children.

Jesus leaves each person free and responsible to make his or her own decisions, as he did when he met the rich young man (cf. Matt. 19:16 ff.). We must never impose our own ideas, but offer them as expressions of love. First and foremost, children are children of God, not ours. We should not treat them, therefore, as our possessions, but as persons who have been entrusted to us.

Correction too is necessary

Jesus does not hesitate to correct, with decision and force when necessary. He says to Peter, who wanted to prevent him from facing his passion: "Get behind me, Satan! . . . for you are setting your mind not on divine things but on human things" (Matt. 16:23). Correction too is necessary. It is an integral part of education: "Those who love them [their children] are diligent to discipline them" (Prov. 13:24), as is written in the sacred book of Proverbs. As father and teacher, God's teaching of the Hebrews consisted in instruction and correction.

Woe to us if we do not correct! We should be guilty of a great omission! This passage from the Prophet Ezekiel is particularly striking: "If . . . you do not speak to warn the wicked to turn from their ways, the wicked shall die in their iniquity, but their blood I shall require at your hand" (Ezek. 33:8). Correction is therefore the duty of parents. Admonishment given with peace, calm and detachment gives children a sense of responsibility. They will remember it.

In the stupendous parable of the prodigal son, Jesus shows us the father's mercy and, therefore, his mercy toward those who repent and return to what is good. Parents must treat their children as God treats us. The mercy of a father and mother in a family must reach the point of knowing truly how to forget, how to "cover over everything" (cf. 1 Cor. 13:7) with God's charity. Repeated reminders of a negative past do not agree with Jesus' way of thinking. This explains why they are not accepted.

Jesus teaches in the synagogue, on the mountain, along the roads of Galilee and Judea, in the temple of Jerusalem. Likewise, any place can be useful to parents for teaching.

Speaking a language that is alive

Jesus' way of expressing himself is new, although he keeps to the customs of his time. He speaks a language that is alive, filled with images, concrete, brief and precise. He avoids any kind of long-windedness. He often condenses into one phrase all that he has to say on a particular subject.

This is what should be done in the family. So-called long "sermons" are not accepted by our young people. A few words are enough, offered by a true, pure and selfless love. Jesus also uses dialogue, alternating questions and answers. He uses maxims, and, with the scribes and Pharisees, discussion.

The dialogue between parents and sons or daughters, whether they be children or adults, must never be interrupted. It must always be open, serene and constructive, as between friends.

There are sons or daughters in many families who turn away from their parents and the faith, despite the gospel witness their parents tried to give. The relationship with these sons and daughters must never be broken no matter which way in life they take, even if they adopt ideologies that are distant from God, even if they become involved with drugs or experiences that contrast radically with the moral teaching they received in the family.

Particularly in the West, we are immersed in a secularized society in which important traditional values have faded away, and new ones have emerged. For example, there is a strong awareness of personal freedom. There is excitement over scientific and technological progress as well as with the overcoming of cultural and national barriers. And there is a different understanding of the role of women in today's society as compared with the past.

Parents must have discernment. While communicating with their children, they must be mindful of the profound changes that have taken place in the context in which their children are living. They need to know how to interpret the "signs of the times" which can be found in some of the new demands expressed by their children.

We must not be afraid

While educating people, Jesus was not afraid to overturn the traditional scale of values, as when he proclaimed the beatitudes (cf. Matt. 5:2). He called "happy," in fact, those who do not appear to be so. He presented a way that is difficult to take, and that is in opposition to what the world offers.

We too must have the courage to state what is truly of value. We must not deceive ourselves, thinking that by presenting a watered-down Christianity and a fictitious Christ, what we propose will be more readily accepted.

God makes himself heard in the hearts of our children. They react in a positive way only to the truth, when it is presented to them with a language that is accessible and acceptable; that is, when it is expressed by parents who, before teaching, have made the effort to understand and to share profoundly in the true demands of the younger generation.

The gospel depicts Jesus speaking "as one having authority" (Matt. 7:29). Parents— trusting in the grace that they have as parents— must never neglect their responsibility as educators. Deep down in their hearts, children require this of them. It is for this very reason that children are often capable of judging their parents ruthlessly if they have been silent about the truth.

Jesus educates by passing on to his disciples "his" typical teaching: "This is my commandment, that you love one another as I have loved you" (John 15:12). By specifying "as I have loved you," Jesus presents himself as the "master" of such love. This must be the teaching *par excellence* that parents give to their children, because it sums up the whole of the gospel. Parents must imitate Jesus so well in their putting it into practice, that they can repeat this commandment to their children as their own: my children, love one another as I have loved you.

Jesus must live in us

Thus, we must imitate Jesus. We must imitate him as teacher. We must imitate Jesus, or better still, we must allow him to live in us. Yes, by far, the best way would be if Jesus himself were to take our place. If he lives in us, our efforts as educators will be beyond reproach. If he becomes the educator in our families, we will carry out our responsibilities perfectly.

Jesus must live in us, he must take our place. How can this come about? The gospel gives us the answer. We were still at the beginning of our new way of life when the Lord urged us to turn it into a divine adventure in which he would be present in us. Then, little by little, implanting in our minds the various ideas that gave rise to the spirituality of unity, the Spirit explained to us how this could become a reality.

Now all those who follow this pathway know how they should act so that Jesus may be in them. We must live the "new self," not the "old self." We must love in a supernatural way, being "outside ourselves," as we say, always overcoming any obstacles that might turn up, by loving Jesus crucified and forsaken. We should not live for ourselves. We must live for the others, "making ourselves one" with them in everything except sin. All these expressions tell us how Jesus can take his place within us.

Jesus was already present in our souls through grace. Now he is more fully present because we co-operate with this grace. Yes, by living in this way, Jesus is in us, Jesus the teacher.

In our midst

But Jesus must also live in the midst of our families. This is the presence of Jesus that comes about in unity, wherever two or more are united in his name (cf. Matt. 18:20). Jesus between husband and wife, between mother and son, between father and daughter, between mother and grandfather or aunt. If Jesus is present among two or more members of our family, his influence as teacher and educator will be greater.

How can we guarantee this precious presence of his in our midst? We know the answer: by nourishing it every day, by rebuilding it whenever it has been shattered, and by keeping ourselves open to one another, indeed, by going out of ourselves toward the other members of our family. I say, going out of ourselves toward the others, because in a family, the first people to love are one's own family members. And this is true no matter what our particular role or place within our movement may be; we know that we must have Jesus as teacher present in our family. The charism of unity urges us to make the family, which is the basic cell of society, into a focolare.[11] This is our specific, characteristic vocation. We become holy to the extent that we aim at doing this.

---

11. The central form of life in the Focolare Movement, a "focolare" is a house in which the members are dedicated to maintaining the presence of Jesus in their midst twenty-four hours a day.

A new generation

Precisely because we have put aside everything, at least spiritually, in order to follow Jesus ("Whoever comes to me and does not hate father and mother, wife and children, brothers and sisters, yes, and even life itself, cannot be my disciple" [Luke 14:26]), we now hear him repeating to us these words: You do not love me if in the first place you do not love your family. Thus, whether we are alone or whether others in our family also live the gospel, Jesus, the teacher, will be present there.

The children who grow up in these families will be a new generation. Together with the life and nourishment they receive from their parents, and with all the affection and assistance that this first social cell offers, they will also be imbued with many of Jesus' ideas— Jesus' evangelical ideas. Consequently, they will grow up reasoning as he reasons. They will learn to see humanity as the great family of God's children. They will no longer believe blindly in other systems; they will believe in the gospel. No relationship will attract them more than that based on Jesus' new commandment. These children will be new.

Thus the divine life received in baptism will be strengthened. Parents will put into action the graces that the sacrament of matrimony has placed at their disposal for the good of their children. Parents will work together with God in the development and up-bringing of God's children.

To educate, to transform the children and the entire family! To make of the family a small church, something dynamic and open to the society around it and to its needs, orienting the children to look beyond themselves, to others and their needs! This is a lofty objective, and in certain cases, it may seem to be unattainable. But we should never despair. On the contrary, we should confidently orient ourselves toward its realization. To understand what we should do, let us look at how the Spirit urged the entire Focolare Movement to act, to make all become one.

Imitate the family of Nazareth

In our Movement, we have welcomed persons of other religions and non-believers. We love these persons as we love ourselves. We joyfully accept their spontaneous commitment to become integral parts of our large family. We share with them all of its spiritual and material patrimony. We are the Focolare Movement because they too are present. Without their presence, we would lose our identity.

It must be like this in our families as well. Whoever is a little distant from one or other Christian ideal, whoever has other ideas or another faith, must be welcomed by us not only with human love, but with supernatural love. We must treasure and appreciate whatever they give to the family, however small it may be. We must know how to highlight the good ideas they have. We must make them share, as much as possible, in the spiritual and material riches of the family. In short, we should do all we can to love this son or daughter or these sons or daughters, so that although they have not yet received the light of faith, in some way they return this love and the family reflects the nature of the Focolare Movement.

Moreover, to make the family a small cell of the Focolare or a small church, which means the same thing, implies imitating the family of Nazareth, that family which lived with Jesus in their midst in the most concrete and divine way. In order to compose this masterpiece, the members of the family of Nazareth loved one another in a supernatural way, which means out of love for God and not for themselves. Mary, who was the true mother of Jesus and true wife of Joseph, loved both of them not for herself, but for God. Joseph did not love Mary for himself. He loved her for God, and he loved the child Jesus for God, even though he was his foster father.

Yes, we must love for God. Our love is truly purified of human attachments if our spirit is always turned toward Jesus forsaken.

My dear friends, I could continue to demonstrate how all the elements of our spirituality are very suitable for guiding the life of the family. But you know it already. Yes, with our Ideal, we can have *the* teacher in our home.

Today, let us renew the resolution of mutual love which makes his presence possible. On this foundation, everything we do today will be meaningful. All the theories and experiences of different teaching methods that are offered to you will also acquire value.

May Our Lady give us many united families for the good of society and of the Church. Through these families we will have, apart from anything else, a powerful means for spreading the kingdom of God in the world.

And by reaching out to other families and to all of humanity the family will become ever more beautiful, more united and more holy. And is this not what God expects from us in an age that demands mature and holy lay people?

Love Builds a Relationship with God

Three thousand people gathered together on 8 April 1989 in Rome, to attend a conference organized by the New Families, based on the theme: "The Family and Prayer."

Chiara Lubich's introduction to her talk on this theme is one that she constantly refers to: the family is experiencing a crisis in the Western world, the result of what is effectively a head-on attack from a consumer and hedonistic society. The same dangers threaten the world elsewhere as current Western values spread and take deeper root in other cultural areas.

We need not lose hope, however, if we know where to look for the ideas and strength that will enable us to overcome our difficulties. We need only to return to the basis from which we should always start. In this case, we must return to the way in which God sees the family: he who is the creator of this fundamental cell within society. Only when this is clearly stated does Chiara feel able to look at the issue of prayer. She does not present a superficial or narrow view of prayer, but one which goes to the heart of the Christian experience. Humankind was created to enjoy a relationship with God. Prayer therefore is the means by which this relationship is expressed, and is continually renewed. Prayer is more than oral and mental conversation with God, but consists in the donation of our whole being: all that makes up the unique relationship we have with our Creator. But prayer, despite being a very intimate matter, is not just individualistic; it builds up the community: "Although Christian prayer is a personal concern, it is also a communal, ecclesial reality." If this is so, then how can it fail to build up the family?

It is only after defining both the family and prayer, however, that Chiara goes on to look at the specific theme of "Prayer and the Family." This puts her in a good position to consider in depth the different means by which, in the family, we can deepen our relationship with God: whether this be through set prayers or a life lived totally for him.

In many ways this talk refers back to ones previously considered. For where there is mutual love lived within the family, there God dwells. What greater prayer can there be than a love which constantly draws the life of the Trinity into the very heart of the family, the "domestic church"?

The Family and Prayer

Our congress, as you know, is entitled: *Family and society: The family rooted in God is open to all humanity.*

Rooted in God. We would like to say something this morning about the relationship that the family has, or should have, with God, the Absolute— so it is a rather special theme. And since this relationship can be defined with one word, prayer, we will speak about *the family and prayer.* It is an important, urgent, demanding and decisive topic which can help the family to carry out its role in a truly effective way. So this talk is like a meditation.

To discuss this theme in depth, however, I think it will be helpful, considering today's society, to begin by looking briefly at the reality of the family. Likewise, it will be useful to reflect on the meaning that prayer generally has in the life of individuals.

The family

The family! Today there is a head-on attack against the family, and the situation seems to be getting worse. The family is threatened, if not destroyed by the decline of traditional moral values, by theoretical and practical materialism, by the hedonistic mentality that grows out of consumerism. And this happens to such an extent that many people are forced to ask: does the family have any meaning, how important is it?

Sociologists, educators, politicians and moralists could offer their opinions. I believe that we Christians are interested above all in trying to understand God's idea of the family, what importance God gives it.

A few basic thoughts will suffice to understand this. First of all, God created the human race with the formation of a family. And when the Word of God came on earth, he willed to be born in a family. Jesus began his public life during the celebration of a new family. God had the family so much at heart, considered it to be of such importance, to impress on it his own image. In fact, the family reflects God's very own life, the life of the Holy Trinity. This is sufficient to say what the family means to God.

What was God's plan for the family? God who is love, thought of the family as an intertwining of relationships of love: nuptial love between the couple, maternal and paternal love for the children, filial love for the parents, the love of grandparents for their grandchildren, of the grandchildren for their grandparents, of children for their uncles and aunts and *vice versa*. The family is therefore a treasure chest, a jewel, a mystery of love.

The family of God

This is how God imagined and how he created the family. And the Son, in redeeming the world, turned this natural love, with which the members of the family are impregnated, into something sublime through the divine love he brought on earth, through the fire that he wants to burn everywhere. Through him, the family has become not only the primary cell of humanity created by God, but also the basic cell of the Church founded by the Son. Because of the supernatural love that the members of the family have for one another— through baptism and the other sacraments, particularly the sacrament of matrimony— they are called individually and collectively to the sublime heights of making the family a small church, an *ecclesiola.*

Turning toward God

And now, something on the meaning of prayer in general. What is prayer? Is prayer important? We might not believe it, or we may never have thought about it, but prayer is something essential to our very being. The reason is that we have been created in the image of God. This means that we have the possibility of being in the presence of God not only as creatures in front of our Creator, but also as the "you" of God: we are capable of establishing a relationship of communion with God. This possibility is so typical of human beings that it constitutes our very nature— it expresses who we really are. We are not truly ourselves if we do not fulfil this specific vocation.

But to grow in our relationship with God, to be in communion with God means to pray. Therefore, only if we pray are we fully as God planned and created us to be.

Our fundamental vocation to prayer becomes evident when we consider people of the most varied religions. Everyone feels inclined to turn toward God or toward a supreme being. In our contacts with brothers and sisters of other religious beliefs, we have discovered texts of prayers that are truly beautiful. They bear witness to the secret but effective action of God who urges people to pray.

Looking at our own experience, we can see that even in our times, in our de-Christianized world, where the focus of life is no longer on God but on human beings (or science, technology and progress), there is a return, a desire, a thirst for prayer, especially among young people. It is a sign that in every epoch our true nature emerges: our being made in the image of God.

But is prayer only a personal concern? While prayer is basically a personal concern, it would be a mistake, especially for us Christians, to consider it only in this way. We are united to one another in the mystical body of Christ. This is a mystery which we can understand to a certain extent by thinking of interconnected containers. When water is placed into one of the containers, the water level increases in all of them. The same thing happens when we pray. Prayer is the elevation of our soul to God, and when we are elevated to him, also the others are elevated. So, although Christian prayer is a personal concern, it is also a communal, ecclesial reality.

This is true always, but it holds true especially for the various expressions of liturgical prayer, which is the apex of Christian prayer because it is the prayer of the Church herself.

I began by giving a few ideas on the family and on prayer so as to better understand both. Now let us look at prayer in the family, at the family's prayer.

Relationship between family and prayer

Is there a relationship between the family and prayer? Does the family have anything to do with prayer? Yes, certainly!

The primary reason is that prayer begins in the family.

It *must* begin in the family. Families are the first schools of prayer. Right from their earliest years, children should begin to perceive a sense of God and worship him. In fact, what we learn as children, also in this field, remains for the rest of our lives. If prayer is not taught in the family, it will be difficult to fill this emptiness later on.

We know that what children learn during the first three years of their lives concerning the supernatural or the divine is essential. Therefore, it is necessary to look after them, especially during their first years and at least until they reach the age of six.

Thus the evangelization of the young, of the world's future, depends largely on the "domestic church," the family.

Parents: bearing witness to God

How can parents effectively carry out their task as teachers of prayer? For children to learn how to pray to God, it is necessary first of all to show them the reality of God. They must discover his existence, know he exists. And here parents have an extraordinary opportunity: they can instill this knowledge into their children by bearing witness to God. "May they all be one" (in love and in truth), Jesus says in the gospel, "so that the world may believe" (cf. John 17:21). May Christians love one another so that the light of faith may radiate in others.

If our mutual love can bring the often unbelieving world of adults, which is fossilized by materialism, secularism and various other evils, to be touched by unity in Christ to the point of making them believe, all the more will the innocent, little world of our children be touched by this witness. It will make them understand that there is Someone who envelops us all with love, and spontaneously they will with confidence turn their minds and hearts to this Someone.

Thus only fathers and mothers who daily live mutual and constant charity, who strengthen and consolidate their human love and transform it into supernatural love, can effectively enter the hearts of their children, leaving traces that future events in life will never be able to cancel.

Models for their children

Mutual love, however, must be put into practice in the right way, so that it responds perfectly to what Jesus commands. Jesus wants a man to see and to love in his wife not only the person with whom he shares his life, but Christ himself in her. In fact, Jesus considers done to him whatever the husband does to his wife and *vice versa*. Furthermore, Jesus in the husband or wife must be loved in the measure that Jesus requires, as he expressed with the words, "Just as I have loved you, you also should love one another" (John 13:34). They must love one another to the point of being ready to give their lives for one another. If parents keep this in mind throughout the day, whether they are praying, working or eating, whether they are resting or studying, laughing or playing with their children, whatever they are doing, every moment will be an opportunity for bearing witness to God.

Not only this, but through their testimony, which demands sacrifice, parents will be more convincing reference points for their children. Jesus said, "And I, when I am lifted up from the earth, [and in some measure this applies to Christians too] will draw all people to myself" (John 12:32). They will become models for their children.

Parents are teachers of prayer

If parents pray together, also making use of external expressions like kneeling down, making the sign of the cross or reciting vocal prayers, the little ones will imitate them. They too will try to kneel down, to make some kind of sign of the cross. Perhaps even in their early years, they will stammer something without understanding anything, but simply led to do so by their parents' example.

Then the time will come to teach them to pray with words. The short prayers that children learn are the beginning of their dialogue with God. Later, as the years pass, children can learn more specific prayers. Parents should take this task to heart. We should remember the grief-stricken invitation of Paul VI to parents: "Mothers, do you teach your children Christian prayers? . . . And you, fathers, do you spend a few moments of prayer with your children, with the entire domestic community? Your example . . . supported by a few common prayers, is worth a lesson of life. It is worth an act of worship of exceptional value."[12] Thus prayer in the family is born and blossoms into a splendid habit.

Praying together united in the name of Jesus

Prayer in the family is a special prayer. It is not like just any other personal prayer. It is exceptionally effective. In fact, Jesus promises to those who are united in his name (and here we assume that the children have been taught to love the rest of the family as the parents do) that he

12. Pope Paul VI, General Audience, 11 August 1976.

himself will be present: "Where two or three are gathered in my name, I am there among them" (Matt. 18:20). He is there to pray with the family, in the family— Jesus himself, the almighty, who can do everything.

And if he is present, how can the Father not listen to him? The family will soon experience God's providence. Faith will grow and with it prayer will be given new value.

How and when to pray

In teaching us to pray, Jesus mentioned two things that may seem to be contradictory, but they are not. He affirmed, "When you pray do not use many words" (cf. Matt. 6:7) and "pray always" (cf. Luke 18:1). Every family should follow these two directives.

Do not use many words. When? During the day there are precise moments in which the family is called to pray. And there are various prayers which Christian piety has taught and teaches for these circumstances. It is not possible to list them here. Perhaps it would be more useful to say what we feel is fundamental in each one.

What is fundamental in the different prayers

When we wake up in the morning, we immerse ourselves in the supernatural world that we entered through baptism, by saying brief prayers to our heavenly Father, to Jesus, to Mary. . . . This is the moment to offer God our entire day. We must love God and to love means to give, so we give him every new day.

Then during the day, involved as we are in worldly

matters (work, study, recreation) it is indispensable for the members of the Christian family, either together or individually, to find the courage to withdraw from the world around them and to devote a few minutes, to "seek," as Saint Paul would say, "the things that are above" (Col. 3:1) to think, that is, to penetrate the world of our faith. This means that we meditate, or as our young people say, that we go "in depth." We should read a passage of scripture, especially from the gospel, and pause to reflect on one point or another which has struck us. Then we can draw from this reading useful resolutions for our life. What is fundamental in this kind of prayer is seriously to put ourselves in contact with God, as children, in order to acquire strength and light.

In the past, also the rosary was said in the family. And this is understandable because by doing so we are able to review the mysteries of our faith every day. We are able to venerate Mary over and over again: "Hail Mary, full of grace . . . blessed are you among women." A person who feels just a little bit of love for Mary willingly says the rosary, because one who loves never tires of saying words of love to the loved one.

The Church still advises us to say the rosary. But if this seems to be too much for us, can we not recite a part of the rosary? Basically, this prayer develops our relationship with one who, in God's plan, is way and door to union with God, who gives us hope, also because she is the mother of a family, and indeed of every Christian family.

In the evening, before going to bed, the family can say another brief prayer together, as in the morning. We can give thanks for our day and also make an act of contrition for the mistakes we have made and resolve to do better the next day.

These are some of the prayers that can be said in the family throughout the day. For those who are able there are many other wonderful things that can also be done, such as going to Church to visit Jesus who is always too alone. And on those days when there is some special need, the family has many chances to gather together and call upon God's help: for the success of an exam, for instance, for the birth of a child, for a sick person in the family, for a financial problem, for the solution to a spiritual crisis. Jesus said, "Ask, and it will be given you; search, and you will find; knock, and the door will be opened for you" (Matt. 7:7). And if he said this, it is true.

The Church's worship

Then there is the eucharist which is the climax of all prayer. On Sunday, the Lord's day, the family, this little church, immerses itself in the Christian assembly that gathers together. The family listens to the word of God. It partakes of the bread and the cup of Christ, and then it extends its eucharistic communion to fraternal communion.

Through the eucharist the members of the family can feel that their hearts are satisfied; they can feel abundant peace.

In fact, we would always want to offer God something fitting to his majesty, something worthy of him. Our offering, however, is so out of proportion to his greatness that it is very consoling to know that in the eucharistic celebration, together with the celebrant, we can offer Jesus himself to the Father. We can offer his sufferings which are of immense value and we can unite our sufferings to his, to adore the Father, to love him, to praise him, to glorify him worthily, to thank him, to ask him for graces and to ask him in a suitable way to forgive our mistakes.

Pray always, pray well

"Do not say many words," but Jesus also tells us "to pray always and not to lose heart" (Luke 18:1).

Pray always. How can we do this? And how can we do this especially in the hectic rush of our daily living? By making every action an act of love for him, possibly preceding every action, as we often do with the more important action, with the words, "For you," as some of the saints have taught.

"To pray always" does not mean that we should multiply our prayers, but that we should direct our hearts and our entire lives to God. We should study for God alone, work and exert every effort, suffer, rest and also die for God alone.

And we should carry out every action in the best way possible, because we know that we can make it an extension of God's creative action and the redemptive action of Jesus toward the achievement of God's plan for the world. Thus all our actions can be transformed into sacred actions.

This way of praying is very much in tune with our times. Today we see the world and all the universe in evolution, and human beings are reminded of their duty to "subdue the earth" (cf. Gen. 1:28). It is especially through this way of praying that we fulfill the command of Jesus: "Pray always" (cf. also Luke 21:36).

Of course, it is also necessary to pray well. We should always begin with a few moments of recollection in order to realize that we are before God. We should pronounce well the words suggested to us by the Church, in order to make them our own and to say them with all our heart. We can also pray spontaneously, confiding to Jesus our innermost secrets. We can tell him how much we want to love him and how much help we need. We can tell him our difficulties, our hopes and plans.

We should pray with faith. "If you have faith and do not doubt . . . even if you say to this mountain. 'Be lifted up and thrown into the sea,' it will be done" (Matt. 21:21).

These are some ideas on prayer in the family. If it is not possible to do everything, which is probably the case, let us do at least something. If we cannot gather together to pray with all the members of the family, let us do so with those who are willing. In any case, there must be prayer in the family. The family as such, especially today, needs the protection of heaven.

Love for others: way to union with God

I would like to add a thought and a suggestion.

In our times, we have, as never before, thousands of forms of stimulation. Day by day we are continually presented with all sorts of amusements, news, images. Television, radio, telephone— so much noise— deafen us. Even without wanting it, even with a degree of control, we are all subject, more or less, to the many sounds that reach our ears. We can hardly help receiving the various ideas supplied by the media. It is difficult to free ourselves from what we could honestly call a bombardment. It is easy to become dominated by these ideas, if not at least attracted by them.

How can we withdraw in order to devote some time

to prayer? Yes, of course, we can use our reason and good will strengthened by faith. But we can also follow the indications of the Holy Spirit, who never ceases to help people of every epoch. We can follow the suggestions he gives precisely for people of our times.

We live in an epoch in which the role of the laity is highlighted in the Church. The laity was the particular object of study during the recent Synod, and the Apostolic Exhortation *Christi Fideles Laici* noted how the Holy Spirit looks at the laity with special love, by enkindling, for example, movements with spiritualities suited to them.

In order to bring the laity to full union with God, these spiritualities do not remove them from their environments. They do not ask them to do hard penances or to fast for long periods in order to guarantee a genuine Christian life. Rather, they encourage the laity to find their way to God right in the midst of the world, where they live shoulder to shoulder with all kinds of people.

These spiritualities emphasize that the heart of Christianity is love for others out of love for Christ, because in this consists the fulfilment of the law. They teach and urge us to live love and to restore it, if it has been shattered, because without such love not even one's offering to God is acceptable. They help us to put love into practice constantly, sharing the fatigues, anxieties, worries and joys with the people we meet in life.

These spiritualities invite the laity to make this love the reason of their lives. And this is the divine wonder: when such committed lay people, fully determined to love the people next to them throughout the day, forgetting about themselves, are recollected in prayer, they find God deep down in their hearts. God invites them to a profound union. They feel loved, and a spontaneous, loving conversation begins. This is a wonderful experience which everyone can have.

What takes place is similar to the life of a plant— the more its roots sink deep into the soil, the higher its stem rises up toward the sky. Here, the more we enter into the hearts of those around us to share in their sufferings and joys, the more our soul rises to union with God.

Conclusion

Are there, indeed, these forces and stimuli in today's society that create a strong attraction toward the outside world, so often made up of vanities that almost hypnotize people and deaden human creativity (in the intellectual sphere, for instance)? Are there forces and stimuli that trap and deceive people by promising easy happiness?

Well, there is also an inner force in the depths of the human heart that attracts people and immunizes them from the spirit of the world. It calls them to a special type of prayer and offers them a peace which the world does not know, joys which are incomparable with those of the world and consolations which fully satisfy them.

May the family, the small lay church, learn to walk along these new ways to reach the Lord that, in our days, the Holy Spirit is indicating. May it learn to experience these sublime effects of love, through which every other prayer in the family acquires new depth. In this way, the family will belong more and more to God, and God will be able to accomplish his plan for the family. He will make it open to many other families, so that all together they may form the vast family of the children of God. They will be linked by the love brought by Jesus and will bear witness to how the entire human family should be in the world.

May Our Lady, singular vessel of devotion, look upon all our families. May she enwrap them with her maternal love. May she make them similar to her family, the holiest family that ever existed or ever will exist— the family with Jesus, her son, and Joseph, her husband.

God's Idea of the Family

The setting for this talk is as extraordinary as the talk itself. On 5 June 1993, in the Olympic Sports Stadium in Rome, Familyfest '93 took place in the presence of twelve thousand people, representing ninety-five different countries from five continents. This event in turn was relayed across the globe through two-way satellite transmissions to simultaneous conferences on the family in Hong Kong, Sao Paulo, Melbourne, Yaounde, Brussels, Buenos Aires and New York. Throughout the world there were also hundreds of other gatherings of people interested in the family tuning in to the satellite signal. The whole event was also broadcast on various major TV networks. It is estimated that this event, celebrating the opening of the United Nations International Year of the Family, was seen by approximately six hundred million people.

To this enormous audience the immensely profound ideas of this talk were launched. It is a prophetic statement and needs to be understood as such. Chiara is speaking about the ideal family, the way God sees the family. Not everyone has a good experience of family life. Families, as so much else in the world, rarely correspond to the ideal. Therefore it is understandable that when Chiara claims: "It is natural for the family to live for the other, to love one another," one is almost tempted to cry out: "Show me a family that really lives like this!" Nonetheless, despite all the failures, there are families that are struggling to live like this.

To enter into the prophetic thought presented here, it is useful to absorb what was said in the talk "The family and love." In fact, the ideas presented here draw upon all that has been said in the previous five talks relating to family life. They provide the context, the background.

Chiara is saying: If the family really lived out its vocation and became what God intended it to be, that is a cell with charity at the core of its existence, then, and only then, could it become a model for the rest of society. Every structure within society is based on relationships, relationships of many kinds. The family is potentially a model for all these relationships. It can illuminate them, showing how they can be lived out in the most efficient, fulfilling and completely human way, when, at the heart of the family, a selfless and mutual love is in action.

Chiara is not being utopian, but visionary in this short, but revolutionary talk. It is an extraordinary piece of work which challenges both the family and society simultaneously. As she concludes: "This is the challenge being offered to you, so that in the Third Millennium, all of humanity may truly become one large family."

Various religious leaders contributed to the Family-fest, through messages of support and encouragement. They show how Chiara's vision is in harmony with the deep intuitions of humanity. The following are a few short extracts.

It takes from three to five generations to change humankind. Families are always the foundation of change. Families are like a field: we must sow good seeds and let them grow. Parents must always live with the awareness that their children look at their behaviour. In Japan there is a saying: "Children grow up watching their parents' backs." This happens in every family. It is also important to view the family in the context of other families; we cannot think only of our own family.

> *The Venerable Etai Yamada,*
> *Supreme High Priest of the Japanese*
> *Tendai Buddhist Federation*

Islam calls upon people to build a society of love and not of hatred and this must take root in the hearts of people: This enables us to have God as our companion for the good of humanity.

> *Imam Barkat, Algeria*

The family is the best terrain given us by God in which the noblest principles and values of life, both of the individual and community, can take root and grow. Within a family, one of the most central and fundamental values is the experience of communion in which everyone shares everything equally, but at the same time this is in harmony with the varying responsibilities of the different members. In this way, while the open market can generate consumers who are insensitive and indifferent to one another, the family can generate these into people who know how to suffer together in solidarity. If "family" above all means "communion" . . . then it is clear that the communion of the Church, which has the life of the most Holy Trinity as its model, must consider the family as the first ideal cell through which to cultivate all the good which derives from the great mystery of communion.

Bartholomew I
Ecumenical Patriarch of Constantinople

And then there is love, the love of God, charity which has been poured into our hearts. It is this outpouring of diving Love, work of the Holy Spirit as you well know, that makes up the spiritual nucleus, the basic nucleus of the family. It is through this love that the family is built, that the family develops, grows, matures, and provides the right conditions with life and love, for the person to find his or her earthly happiness, journeying towards eternal happiness, through family communion.

Pope John Paul II

Seeds of Hope: The Family as a Model for Humanity

A warm greeting to all of you who are present at the Palaeur Stadium in Rome, to the families participating in more than five hundred other congresses linked with us in five continents, and to all those who are watching or listening to the Familyfest via television and radio.

We are at the threshold of the third millennium. The family, every family, can play an important role in this period of history. The family, invented by God as the masterpiece of love, can inspire the guidelines which will contribute toward changing the world of tomorrow.

In fact, if we explore the family, if we take an X-ray of it, we can discover immense and very precious values which, when extended and applied to the whole of humanity, can transform it into one large family.

The family is founded on love

The family is founded on love, a bond that has many facets: love between husbands and wives, between parents and children, between grandparents, between aunts and uncles and nieces and nephews, between brothers and sisters. It is a love that constantly grows and goes beyond its own boundaries. Love between husband and wife generates new life, and love between brothers and sisters becomes friendship. Authority and roles within the family, because they are expressions of love, are naturally recognized.

A family naturally puts everything in common, shares all its goods, and has just one family budget. Savings are not the result of hoarding money but provision for the future. It is normal to meet the needs of those who do not yet earn their living as well as those who can no longer do so.

In a family, people of all ages live together; it is natural to live for the other person, to love one another.

Education too happens spontaneously if we think of a child's first steps and first words. Correction is given only for the good of the person.

A sense of justice is normal in a family, and it is normal for each member to feel the guilt and shame experienced by another. Likewise, it is natural to suffer and sacrifice oneself for the others, to carry one another's burdens. Solidarity and faithfulness to the family are spontaneous.

In a family, the life of the other person is as precious as your own, sometimes even more so. Each one is concerned about the health of the others and looks after whoever is unwell.

The family is the natural setting where life begins and ends and where the disabled, the elderly and the terminally ill find acceptance, affection and care.

Each family member is nourished and dressed according to his or her need.

The home is created and cared for together by all the members of the family.

Both teaching and learning take place in the family and everything contributes toward the development of the person. Family members may have different cultural values, but every diversity becomes a source of enrichment for all.

Communication too comes naturally in a family, each member participating in everything and sharing everything.

Passing on values

The task of every family is to live its vocation as a family so perfectly that it becomes a model for the whole human family. It should pass on its own values through its characteristic way of being.

In this way, the family will become, as the title of the Familyfest says, a seed of communion for humanity of the third millennium.

Seeds of a new world

Is it natural for the family to put everything in common? Well then, this is the seed that in society can develop into an economy at the service of the human person. It is the seed for a culture of giving, for an economy of communion.

Is it natural in the family to live for the other, to feel the others life as one's own, "to live the other"? Here we have the seed of acceptance among groups, peoples, traditions, races and civilizations that opens the way to mutual inculturation.

Are values spontaneously passed on in the family, from one generation to the next? This could stimulate a new understanding of education in society, and the family's manner of correcting and forgiving could enlighten our judicial systems.

Is the life of each family member as precious as one's own? This is the seed for that culture of life which must permeate laws and social structures.

Does the family care for its home and does the home reflect family harmony? Here we have the seed of renewed sensitivity toward the environment and ecology.

Is education viewed by the family as a means for helping its members to mature? This is the seed that can gradually lead cultural, scientific and technological research to discover God's mysterious plan for humanity and to work for the good of the whole human family.

Is communication in the family impartial and constructive? This is the seed for a social communications system at the service of the person, which highlights what is positive and is an instrument of peace and global unity.

Is love the natural bond among the members of a family? This is the seed for structures and institutions which must co-operate for the good of the community and of individuals and build universal brotherhood by showing appreciation for every people.

Some local, national and international structures and institutions with these objectives already exist in the world: government offices, hospitals, schools, courts of law, banks, associations and various kinds of organizations. But these structures need to be humanized, to be given a soul. It is to the family then that we must look. The spirit of service must reach the same intensity, the same spontaneity, and the same spirit of love for each individual as in the family.

God created the family as an example and a model for every other form of human community. The task of families then is to keep the flame of love always alight in their homes. In this way they will revive the values God gave to the family and bring them generously and unceasingly into society.

This is the challenge being offered to you so that in the third millennium all of humanity may truly become one large family.